MW00626393

GOOD THINGS

COME FROM

HARD TIMES

Featuring Advice from Conversations with Leading Executives

By Keith Daniel Washo

Published Author of "The Heart of Success"

QUOTES AND TESTIMONIALS

"Good Things Come From Hard Times is filled with wise advice on succeeding in relationships and life. These helpful tools will change your perspective in a powerful way."

—Dorie Clark, adjunct professor at Duke University's Fuqua School of Business and author, Entrepreneurial You, and Stand Out

"If you're seeking help in overcoming adversity and looking for a good perspective to get you through any challenges this book is an insightful read that can help your mind, heart, and soul "

—Dr. Matt Capuano, family medicine doctor in Rochester, New York and affiliated with Jupiter Medical Center.

"This book is a must read for anyone desiring better life skills and a road-map for overcoming adversity. Washo's book is loaded with great advice and countless practical principles to apply directly to your life that will make a difference in getting you through any challenges"

—Brennan Farrell, Author "The Smart Business" and Principal of VAL 3 Solutions

Good Things Come from Hard Times

ISBN-13: 978-0-692-16821-9

Edited by: Geoffrey Stone

Book Cover Design by: Janelle Keller

Printed in the United States of America

First Printed: October 2018

ACKNOWLEDGEMENT

This book is dedicated to my colleagues in Silicon Valley, Research Triangle Park, and all the executives who participated in this book. To my classmates from State University of New York at Oswego, University of Miami, and Saint Mary's College of California. Additionally, to all my friends and family who supported me throughout the years.

Furthermore, this book is dedicated to my Mother, Ceil Washo. Thanks for always believing in me, loving, and caring with all your heart. Thank you, Janelle Keller for your love, support, faith, and encouragement.

Lastly, this book is dedicated to you the reader. I hope this book serves as a guiding light and helpful resource to getting you through challenges in life. I hope it instills in you faith and confidence plus shows you a light at the end of the tunnel to move forward knowing good things come from hard times.

"We know that all things work for good for those who love God, who are called according to his purpose." **Romans 8:28**

THESIS

Thesis: A statement or theory that is put forward as a premise to be maintained or proved.

This book proposes good things come from hard times. That every challenge you face can be received as a gift. Knowing adversity provides you a special seed to plant that with the right care and actions can blossom beautifully and fruitfully to produce a better you, a better life, and better future.

This book shares with you how good things come from getting through adversity and how hard things you face actually make for an easier better life in the future. That for every perceived negative situation with the right outlook and effort can be viewed as positive and transformative to producing fruitful outcomes. Indeed many gifts and joy to be had from the experiences and learning granted through our challenges.

In the pages ahead you will enjoy wisdom shared from executives who walked the walk facing both personal and professional struggles in which when overcoming the adversity proved to be a blessing in disguise. Getting up, over, and through obstacles provided fertile ground for becoming a bigger, better, wiser, and stronger. It can and will happen to you too! Believe!

TABLE OF CONTENTS

FOREWORD

by Shelda Abdur Razzaq (MA,LPC,CEAP)

Licensed Professional Counselor and Certified Employee Assistance Professional

This book is a personal labor of love where Keith Washo aims to help you overcome hard times with a healthy mindset and have good advice that can lead you through challenges. You are invited to join Keith in his aim to share with you a helpful perspective on how good things come from hard times. You get to listen in on his conversations with executives he admires as he uncovers lessons from their experiences. He distills advice further to get to the bottom line with his wisdom, often presented gently with his graphic art spread throughout the book.

Keith covers not only perspectives on getting through hard times, but also advice on overcoming and keeping the faith. In this account of Keith's sincere distillation, based on his search, you may find your own answers to support your journey toward overcoming challenges and becoming a better you.

Keith's mission is to pass on wisdom based on interviews of executives, related quotes from readings, and his own personal experiences. Here is a wonderful way to learn through his words, straight from his head, heart, and hands. His book is not a one size fit all, but an empowering resource that can aid each of us.

About Shelda Abdur-Razzaq

Shelda Abdur Razzaq graduated with a Masters of Art degree in Counseling from North Carolina Central University. She is Licensed with the State of North Carolina and currently the owner of Triangle Associates for Wellness, PLLC and has been in private practice 20+ years. She specializes in Cognitive Behavioral (CBT), Mindfulness-based (MBCT), Solution Focused Brief (SFBT). Shelda is also a Licensed Employee Assistance Professional.

CONTRIBUTORS

- Andrew Schwab, President of First Flight Venture Center
- Bob Witter, CEO of Device Solutions
- Chris Heivly, Managing Partner of The Startup Factory
- Craig Stone, CEO of Hire Networks
- David Gardner, Founder of Cofounders Capital
- Eric Wagner, CEO of Brueprint Brewing
- John Rosar, CEO of RevGen
- Kerri Hall, CEO of MicMag by Me
- Mark Bavisotto, Founder of Successive Technologies & Startup Summit
- Mark Steele, President of SPMC Group
- Dr. Steven LeBoeuf, President and Co-founder of Valencell
- Sumit Vohra, CEO of Lonerider Brewery
- Will Barfield, CEO of Barfield Revenue Consulting
- Sean Patrick Tario, CEO of Open Spectrum

PREFACE

This book aims to encourage you to get through hard times and give you actionable insights to overcome any obstacles and realize there is a light at the end of the tunnel. I personally had to overcome adversity that inspired the writing of this book per my own challenges losing my father relatively early, a failed relationship, moving to new cities to start new careers in uncharted waters, working new jobs in new industries that we're outside my comfort zone, and launching my own company. I knocked and sought to find advice from smart experienced good wise people and happy to share the insights for you to help you're journey. To offer you this wisdom and advice I assembled an accomplished group of executives who have faced hard times throughout their life both professional and personal. I selected these executives for three main reasons. First, they are great leaders of both companies and families so had to juggle a lot in their colorful life experiences to overcome challenges along the way. Second, all the executives I interviewed are people I got to know personally and meet in the Research Triangle Park, North Carolina region. And lastly, I sought out executives who have been successful in their careers despite odds and challenges along the way, but most importantly shine a light as good people who triumphed and became better human beings having been through tough times.

The executives and their colorful life journeys remind me of the quote from Theodore Roosevelt. This is from the speech "Citizenship in a Republic" he delivered at the Sorbonne, in

Paris, France on April 23, 1910:

> It is not the critic who counts; not the
> man who points out how the strong
> man stumbles, or where the doer of
> deeds could have done them better.
> The credit belongs to the man who
> is actually in the arena, whose face is
> marred by dust and sweat and blood;
> who strives valiantly; who errs, who
> comes short again and again, because
> there is no effort without error and
> shortcoming; but who does actually
> strive to do the deeds; who knows
> great enthusiasms, the great devotions;
> who spends himself in a worthy cause;
> who at the best knows in the end the
> triumph of high achievement, and who
> at the worst, if he fails, at least fails
> while daring greatly, so that his place
> shall never be with those cold and timid
> souls who neither know victory nor
> defeat.

You can understand the reason why I chose these good leaders when you read the biography section at the end of this book. It gives you more depth on who these executives are and where they are today. I'm confident based on the executive insights shared throughout the book and my supporting information you'll gain great practical advice on getting through hard times and have new vigor coupled with hope that blessings awaits you as you walk through your rainy days toward sunshine ahead. A special thanks to all the executives for their wisdom and advice. This book became possible because these executives took time to meet with me personally for lunch or coffee and share their knowledge and life experiences. Thanks to these executives, this book will enrich you and serve as a guiding light towards your own personal upward and onward climb!

INTRODUCTION

When you examine some of the most successful people like renowned greats Steve Jobs, Albert Einstein, Walt Disney, Winston Churchill, J. K. Rowling, Thomas Edison, and Oprah Winfrey you find they went through many failures — both professionally and personally — before their greatest achievements. The lives of many of the most remarkable people went through low valleys to hit mountain tops prove that great things arise from challenging life experiences.

In these pages, I share with you how successful people faced adversity and overcame obstacles, what they did to rise above the challenges, and the valuable lessons and personal growth gained along the way that resulted in blessings both professionally and personally. May this book help you overcome hard times and gives you that extra confidence boost to know that wonderful fruits come from over-coming life's challenges.

By combining leading executives' advice and personal research and anecdotes about converting setbacks into future success, may you enjoy a refreshing view on how good things come from hard times. Be encouraged, build up your faith and confidence, and march forward with personal improvement steps that will deliver you greater success. May this advice on overcoming challenges, finding strength, building resilience, and understand-ing that great things are gifted through perse-vering give you fuel to push forward and rise up. If you implement the wisdom shared, you will be a better person and enjoy new found blessings and success. Believe! Good things re-ally do come from hard times.

Wishing you courage and strength through any dark nights and new lighted path to green-er pastures ahead! You can do it! Lets begin!

PART ONE:

Understanding Challenging Times

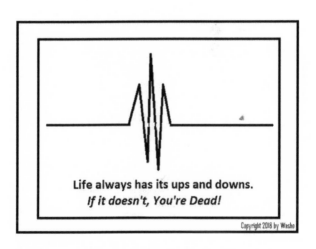

Life always has its ups and downs.
If it doesn't, You're Dead!

Copyright 2018 by Washo

Part One helps you have a good perspective on life so you can view the ups and downs in your journey with the right mind-set. As this picture portrays, if you're not experiencing ups and downs, you're dead. Just like a stock market or roller coaster, our lives are colored with highs and lows. Life is not rainbows and unicorns. Yes, it can be hard at times, but sometimes having our rose-colored glasses shattered is exactly what we need to see more clearly, to see the true vibrant colors of this world. So say amen to down times as it proves you're alive and lets you see and experience the world in more vibrant color. The quality of any situation depends on how you look at it, so remember the glass is always half full. Enjoy these chapters about having a good outlook on this precious thing called life and relish in the keys to overcoming adversity along your journey. Keep your mind open to the fresh and distinctive new ways of dealing with adversity in the message ahead.

CHAPTER 1

HAVE A GOOD PERSPECTIVE AND RIGHT MIND-SET

"No Pain, No Gain"- Rocky Balboa

Perhaps one of the most cliché phrases in history made famous in the movie *Rocky* starring Sylvester Stallone is "No pain, no gain." Rocky shouted repeatedly while training, "No pain, no gain!" These four words capture the essence of working out and fitness. You feel pain when your body is pushed to the breaking point and muscle fibers tear, but it's through this pain that your body produces new healthy muscles resulting in a bigger stronger you. It's through your pain that you gain strength. This phrase can also be a motivator to you. I remember as a kid working out and training for my soccer and tennis teams. When I was feeling tired and wanted to quit I would shout to myself, "No Pain, No Gain" and it would pump me up. Saying the phrase alone would motivate me to push on and keep going. It would also bring some laughter as when training with my brothers we would shout it to each other with a smile in which always gave a good laugh and extra positive spirit push to keep training. Give it a try. Next time your down or feel like giving up, look in the mirror and shout with a smile,

"No Pain, No Gain". Watch the movie Rocky and see how it can help you rock on!

Another spin on this quote is, "Pain is weakness leaving the body." Either way, pain can be good and lead to newness and extra strength. This simple truth demonstrated by the physical manifestation of pain in our body is similar to our spiritual, emotional, and life journey too. Without things in life that evoke some pain in our journey, there is no significant growth achieved. Think about it. Through the pain of labor a beautiful child is born, bringing immense joy. Through the pain of an illness we learn to totally appreciate our wellness. Through the pain of a current job path we feel the angst to move on to a different job or career that leads to more fulfillment. Without salt there is no enjoyment of sweet. Without clouds there is no appreciation for sun. Without cold there is no love for warmth. Everything goes hand in hand like yin and yang. In the famous yin-yang symbol challenge and opportunity come together in one circle. This teaches us that every challenge carries with it an equal and opposite direct opportunity. And so it goes with this beautiful thing we call life. Will Barfield, CEO of Barfield Revenue Consulting, shared his thoughts on this perspective:

> "We all go through hard times and challenges. This is what shapes us. It can be scary going through adversity, but it's what causes growth and strength, like training. You need to tear muscle to repair to build a stronger you. Don't succumb to the negative. See the other side. See the light at the end of the tunnel and commit to fighting your way towards the light."

The first thing to understanding about challenging times is to realize that they are normal. They are part of life. Think about it, Scripture clearly teaches we will have struggles. The Apostle James wrote that we should consider it all joy "when you encounter various trials". (James 1:2) Please note Saint James did not say *if* we encounter trials, but clearly when you have trials as a strong point made of being very clear we will have trials as part of life. He went on to say that we should consider it joy when we have these trials because the "testing of your faith produces perseverance" (James 1:3). Isn't the production of perseverance a great thing? We would all love to have more perseverance to help us push through anything right? Well the testing gifted to us through hard times makes us have to practice our faith that things can and will get better to progress through the challenge in which then builds up a deeper well of perseverance in us. A deeper well of perseverance is a great gift to receive. The Apostle Paul also talks about the extra gain that comes from these trials. He wrote that we should "boast of our afflictions, knowing that affliction produces endurance, and endurance, proven character, and proven character, hope, and hope does not disappoint" (Romans 5:3-5). Clearly in this teaching our afflictions create a basketful of gifts with better endurance, character, and hope. This is a buy one get three free! In addition, in Pauls' second letter he wrote that we should "boast most gladly of [our] weaknesses," for when we are weak, then we are strong (2 Corinthians 12:9-10). This is eye opening wisdom because our traditional thinking and culture today would have us think weakness is weak, but note the opposite effect. When we are weak we are strong because it's in recognizing our weakness our new found humble nature sees the need for change, faith, and right action to move forward living a better path. We are stronger now for this weakness.

Trials and tribulations come with both a purpose and reward. Trials develop good character and enables us to move forward bigger, better, and stronger. Founder and CEO of Hobby Lobby, David Green shared this summary on his own experience with hard times:

> I have learned that many successful business owners tell stories through the years, and a surprising truth seems to

surface in nearly all of their experiences. It is true that the hard times were often when they learned the lessons that took them from good to great. They took the time to "mine the valley" to learn the lessons the bitter seasons had to teach. Because they did, they rose to greatness on the strength of character and wisdom they never would have had without the benefits of hardships.

One of the best lines in the quote above from David Green at Hobby Lobby is that the businessmen took "time to mine the valley." That's a great metaphor for understanding that in our low points, when we're walking through the valley of life, it's in these exact lower valleys where we can best mine for great treasures. The bottom of the gorge are where all the best gold and oil resides. So take the time to mine these fertile low points to seize the treasures that lie beneath. Understand that hard times are a part of life and the best growth happens through them.

Andrew Schwab, President of First Flight Venture Center shared something relative to this theme:

> Recognize that your life journey has ups and downs. Recognize that life is a challenge and struggle part of our human condition. Think of life like a balance sheet with positives (+) and negatives (-). Just try your best to be in the positive as much as you can and be grateful for when you are and recognize you can get back to more positive with the right efforts when you have any setbacks.

This accounting view of your life journey is a distinctive view and supports a new way of dealing with adversity. We all have debits and credits, so just do your best to give back to others and receive more positive column checks. Be thankful for all the credits in your life. Whenever you get a few debits (negatives) in your journey just take the time to learn from them and then take actions that lead to more credits (pluses) on your balance sheet — whether giving back to others, working out for good fitness and health, investing in your education, or working hard on something you love. In a way be a good banker and investor with your life bank account. Manage your life currency well and live well!

Another good perspective is what Mark Steele, CEO of SPMC Group, shared:

> Be opportunistic. Even when the skies are dark, know the sun is shining above those clouds. The sun will shine again. When in the rain, know it will pass. No matter what dark or challenging time in you can always change you point of view and see the sun above those clouds. Focus on the positive.

This fresh perspective reminds me of faith. Faith is believing in the unseen. Just because you can't see the sun on a cloudy day, it's still shining and we can have faith knowing that the sun is above. And remember even on a cloudy day you can still get a good sun tan because those sunbeams are still coming through the clouds so keep a "glass half full" outlook because truly your cup is always half full. One of my favorite funny quotes on life always ½ good by default is when I asked a work-mate how he was doing. He replied, "Still vertical so all good". Classic simple good mindset to keep a healthy perspective. If we can stand vertical and walk, it's already a great day!

Another distinctive perspective on how it's okay if you're having down times per the normal ebbs and flows of life is what Sumit Vohra, CEO of Lonerider Brewery, communicated:

> Understand that life and things we endure can sometimes be harder than we think. We don't live in a perfect world. People are not perfect. Companies are not perfect. Everything is imperfect so it just makes things a little harder.

This is a great reality check because if we accept this imperfect world with imperfect outcomes, we can cope better with any disappointment or frustration. The sooner we understand that not everything is sunshine and rainbows, the sooner we will have healthier and more reasonable expectations. If things don't go as smooth as planned, then accept it calmly, act on it to make things better, and move on. Don't wallow or cry "poor me" if things don't go your way. And if things do go smoothly, give praise and thanks knowing it's a blessing. The point is be ok knowing life isn't always ok. Life is perfect even though it's imperfect. It's through imperfections we can appreciate the beauty in perfections and aspire for perfections in ourselves as we strive for greatness.

It's always good to have the right perspective and realistic mind-set that life, while magnificently beautiful and a gift indeed, isn't always going to be easy. Andrew Schwab, President of First Flight Venture Center, shared this mentality from a business perspective:

Understand that in business or a startup it can be a street fight. Not always a gentleman's game. We all go through lows, so we need to fight through the hard times to survive and then be poised to thrive. . . One of the challenges of going through hard times is the uncertainty factor. You need to recognize that is okay to have uncertainty. It's part of life, and you must move forward through it. The best way through uncertainty is to not rely on any one thing. Hang your hat on many opportunities and hedge your bets to diversify yourself. You never know which opportunity will blossom so plant seeds in many areas.

This is super practical advice on having the right mind-set with a realistic expectation so you can ride the highs and ride out the lows. It is also very good tactical advice on how to push through the lows by doing things that lead to new outcomes. Do many things as you never know which action will bring you up and over! Ever hear that saying "lets' throw things at the wall to see what sticks?" Or "lets try the shotgun approach." This is solid advice around trying and testing many things to experience and learn what works best as you never really know what will produce the best result in life's uncertainty. So the one thing that is certain is that something good certainly comes from trying various things as you work through challenges.

A good quote that summarizes accepting life's ups and downs is:

> Be thankful for the difficult times. During those times, you grow. Be thankful for your limitations, because they give you opportunities for improvement. Be thankful for each new challenge, because it will build your strength and character. Be thankful for your mistakes. They will teach you valuable lessons." (Troy Amdahl, work-

life balance expert and one of the Oola guys found at Oolalife.com)

Isn't this quote beautiful? The point is be thankful. We have so much to be thankful for when you look for the blessings around you. Every night before you go to bed think about what you're thankful for. You will see that many of your gratitudes come from how you did positive work to get through things and that made you happy and a better person.

One of my favorite perspectives on how hard times is part of life and how good things come from these times was shared by David Gardner, managing partner of Cofounders Capital. He shared this wonderful poem by Robert Browning Hamilton:

I walked a mile with pleasure;

She chatted all the way;

But left me none the wiser

For all she had to say.

I waked a mile with sorrow;

And ne'er a word said she;

But, Oh! The things I learned from her,

When sorrow walked with me."

This poem provides the wonderful truth that we learn and grow much more through hard times. That challenges become our greatest teachers and provide the best learning moments. These teachable moments that happen in the valley can be our greatest instructors providing the best wisdom. With that perspective the lessons learned during harder times can truly be seen as gifts to cherish.

David Gardner told me, "If we know we'll have a difficult road and bumps on our path at times, then all the bumps in the road tells us that we're on the right path." I love this perspective as it wonderfully reframes how setbacks along our journey are part of what is to be expected as we walk through life. Most of the best product ideas, services, or relationships often encountered "bumps in the road." How many times have you heard of couples who almost didn't make it? Or a company that almost went bankrupt? Or an athlete who almost quit, but when putting things into perspective and being strong, resilient, and pushing to overcome, big things emerged. Remember a brilliant diamond is nothing more than a piece of coal that stuck to its job!

To highlight this viewpoint on challenges being par for the course in life, David Gardner provided this wonderful fishing analogy:

> If you think of a nice day fishing and you go out to cast a line and no fish bite, you don't get sad or complain or think you failed. You're not failing at all, you are fishing! We all know part of the fishing process is not catching fish! So we adjust our course, try a new lure, try a new fishing area, or new technique till we catch a fish. With this perspective it's

easy to see how life is full of beautiful days and sometimes less rosy days, but that's okay. It's normal. Just enjoy the good moments and then do our best to get through the down times in doing anything we can to push forward toward sunshine. And remember, "All sunshine makes a desert" so enjoy the rain at times. Like this famous saying, "Life isn't about waiting for the storm to pass. It's about learning to dance in the rain."

When I met with Dr. Steven LeBoeuf, founder and president of Valencell, for lunch after moving to Raleigh and interviewed him about his life journey, he reflected on some hard times he experienced getting through school, his first corporate job, and starting his own company. Dr. LeBoeuf shared this good basis of understanding:

Realize in life there are always challenges needing to be overcome.

Know the hard times are just fuel to propel you to success and push you to do more, be better. Learn to have peace in the moment and be present. Be present and enjoy your hard times as seeing them as good growth moments. Also, understand when in a hard spot or with your back against the wall, it forces you to be creative and find a way to push yourself beyond your limits.

A great highlight from this feedback is the perspective that "hard times are fuel to propel you to success." Just like a rocket needs fuel to boost out of orbit, we too need fuel to break through our ruts and atmospheres. The challenges we face can be seen as the fuel we need to break free from anything holding us back from bigger better endeavors and/or personal growth opportunities.

One of the most powerful lines I have found that gives an amazing metaphor for a healthy perspective on hard days came from author Barbara Haines Howett: "Just when the caterpillar thought the world was over, she became a butterfly." The key is to keep the right perspective and keep the faith. Things do and will get better in proper time. Kerri Hall, CEO of MicMag by Me, shared this lovely outlook: "Our life path is not always a traditional way or straight line. You can create your own path. God writes straight through crooked lines. Understand the hills and valleys are part of life."

This is a wonderful reminder that life isn't always about this perfect chart of progress. Life is not like the perfect sales growth curve: up and to the right. It is more like a stock market graph that goes through ups and downs along the journey of an upward climb. You never really know how a situation can lead to something and be part of a bigger plan. This reminds me of a two-thousand-year-old story from the Taoist tradition about a farmer and his horse that teaches us not to judge our moments as good or bad as you never really know the full meaning or implication of a situation:

One day a farmers' horse runs away. And his neighbor comes over and says, to sympathize, "I'm so sorry about your horse." And the farmer says, "Who Knows What's Good or Bad?" The neighbor is confused because this is clearly not a good thing. The horse is the most valuable animal he owns.

But the horse comes back the next day and he brings with him twelve royal horses. The neighbor comes back over to celebrate, "Congratulations on your great fortune!" And the farmer replies again: "Who Knows What's Good or Bad?"

And the next day the farmer's son is training one of the wild horses, and he's thrown and breaks his leg. The neighbor comes back over, "I'm so sorry about your son." The farmer repeats: "Who Knows What's Good or Bad?"

Just a few hours later, the very next day the army comes through their village and is pulling able-bodied young men to go and fight in war, but the son is spared because of his broken leg. When the neighbor comes in to say how fortunately everything had turned out, he said, "May be."

And this story can go on and on for all causes. Good. Bad. Who knows?

But what's the moral of the story? Well, the meaning of that story is that the paradigm in which we label experiences good or bad is wrong. It's a false dichotomy. The distinction between good and bad is not as clear as black and white; it's blurry and gray.

The Taoist have another way of symbolizing "What's Good or Bad" and it's in the yin and yang symbol. We see black and white, right and wrong, good and bad, but it's fluid. One is melting into the other, even contained inside the other. These things aren't contradictory, they're complimentary. They're two parts of a greater whole. **There is just what is.** It's neither good or bad; there are two sides. Again, always look for the glass half full.

Former president Richard Nixon remarked upon leaving the White House, "Only if you have been in the deepest valley, can you ever know how magnificent it is to be on the highest mountain." This relates to the depth of our appreciation for things and how our ability to feel gratitude, thankfulness, and joy grows to a bigger mountain each time we experience any valley. In order to truly know and appreciate the highs you must know the lows.

When I interviewed Craig Stone, CEO of Hire Networks, he shared a short and sweet phrase his father taught him that helped Craig be more awake and aware of life's twists and turns: "If things are going really well, be ready." This simple phrase helped capture the truism that life is full of challenges and hard times. That is life. Reality. So be ready for the ups and downs. And when things are great, cherish it because not all days go superbly. Be ready in case things change. It's healthy to be mindful of this. Just keep the mind-set that on the flipside when things turn a little gray, know it's going to get better. Have faith. Hard times are a part of life and temporary. Keep things in perspective and be lighthearted. Don't always take things so seriously. Life really is short. As they say, "here today, gone tomorrow." As Eric Wagner, CEO of Brüeprint Brewery, said with a smile, "If you're having a bad day, tomorrow will be better. If tomorrow is not better, than your day was not so bad after all." This is a fun quote to remind us to always keep things in perspective. It's never as bad as we think something is, and it could always be worse.

Many times when we hear about people going through hard times we hear the phrase, "rock bottom." It was at that moment I hit "rock bottom." Have you ever notice how hitting rock bottom for many of the greats provided the springboard they needed to make a significant leap forward? J. K. Rowling, author of the best-selling Harry Potter books, went years living on welfare and being unknown. She hit rock bottom after not being able to find a publisher for any of her works. It was in this lowest time that she had the idea for Harry Potter. Rowling said, "Rock bottom became the solid foundation on which I rebuilt my life." Can you think of a more beautiful way to look at the hard times in your life and see all the lows as golden opportunities to lead to new highs?

The secret to staying positive during hard times is having a good mind-set. According to Sean Patrick Tario, CEO of Open Spectrum

> The key mind-set is to view every challenge as an opportunity. Every hard time is a catalyst to learn something new, grow, push through, and become stronger. Going through hard tough times and sticking through things

makes you stronger and better. It's easier to get through future challenges having overcome things previously and getting through challenges builds more confidence. Lastly, know that you have a higher calling and were meant to do great things. Just learn through failure.

It is important to keep a high view of your situation so you can look down on it with the right perspective. Meaning don't make a mountain out of molehill and know this too shall pass. Another way to adhere to a good mind-set is to not get so bogged down in the minutia. As they say to athletes preparing for a competition, "Keep your eye on the prize."

Finally, a good perspective is realizing you're unique and have a special opportunity to blaze your own trail and let your life shine in the way only yours can. When interviewing Will Barfield, CEO of Barfield Revenue Consulting, he brought up the famous Frank Sinatra song, "My Way" that ties this point home. Will said, "You have to make your own unique path and be you. Do it your way. Yes, talk to stakeholders and advisors and calibrate where needed, but in the end, go for it. Be you and do you!" Sumit Vohra, CEO of Lonerider Brewery also shared a point about this perspective of seeing your unique self-shining in life through all the ups and downs in your own way. Sumit said, "Remember your time is limited. Don't live someone's life. You have to live your own." He then referred to one of his favorite quotes by Steve Jobs:

> Your time is limited, so don't waste it living someone else's life. Don't be trapped by dogma — which is living with the results of other people's thinking. Don't let the noise of others' opinions drown out your own inner voice. And most important, have the courage to follow your heart and intuition.

This is a great quote to share as we need to remind ourselves we have only one life to live, and your short precious life is this world's only time to see your uniqueness shine. You have to be you and do you. Isn't the world more blessed when you are 100 percent yourself? Ever here this quote that hits this point home? "Always be a first-rate version of yourself, instead of a second-rate version of somebody else." Can I get an amen?

Hopefully by now this chapter helps you fully grasp and be at peace knowing that hard times are part of life. It's okay to embrace them as part of the normal life journey. There is a time and place for everything. One of the best Scripture passages that captures all the time and seasons for everything in our life is Ecclesiastes 3. Embrace these words to help with your high-level understanding and perspective as you walk through the seasons of your life. It's the seasons that make the year so wonderfully new, ever-changing, fresh, and beautiful. Take all in stride!

There is an appointed time for everything,

and a time for every affair under the heavens.

time to give birth, and a time to die;

a time to plant, and a time to uproot the plant.

time to kill, and a time to heal;

a time to tear down, and a time to build.

time to weep, and a time to laugh;

a time to mourn, and a time to dance.

time to scatter stones, and a time to gather them;

a time to embrace, and a time to be far from embraces.

time to seek, and a time to lose;

a time to keep, and a time to cast away.

time to rend, and a time to sew;

a time to be silent, and a time to speak.

time to love, and a time to hate;

a time of war, and a time of peace.

(Ecclesiastes 3:1-8)

Chapter 1 Reflection

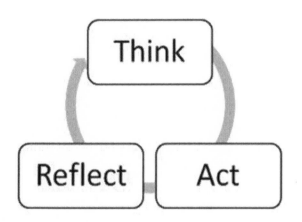

"I am convinced that life is 10% what happens to me and 90% of how I react to it. And so it is with you... we are in charge of our Attitudes."

— *Charles R. Swindoll*

What stands out fresh and distinctive to you from this chapter on having a good perspective and right mind-set?

How can you deal with adversity in a new way based on the teachings from this chapter?

PART ONE:

Overcoming

In the previous section we reviewed how important it is to have a good positive perspective and right mind-set for dealing with any hard times in life. Like this picture above shows a hard brick wall can be overcome with your right spirit and efforts. Now that we understand and embrace challenges as a normal part of our journey and good for our overall growth, let's look at how we can best manage down times to ensure we are learning and growing in the best way possible. In this section, I share with you advice on overcoming and moving forward.

You will learn the importance of surrounding yourself with good people and how it's wise to ask for help. In addition, you will learn why it's critical to write things down, have a plan, and then take that first step. Lastly, you will learn why it's important to take care of yourself and never give up—to make it through

SURROUND YOURSELF WITH GOOD PEOPLE AND ASK FOR HELP

You're The Average Of The 5 People You Spend The Most Time With....

"Surround yourself with good people. People who are going to be honest with you and look out for your best interests." – Derek Jeter

When one of the best baseball players in New York Yankee history with one of the most noble careers says it's important to surround yourself with good people, it's best to heed his advice. Derek Jeter did not become the best ball player in the league by himself. No man is an island. Surrounding yourself with positive people who have your best interest at heart, are honest with you, and lift you up is critical to your overall character and success in life, especially during hard times. You need positive people around you who extend their hand to help lift you up, not negative people who kick you while you're down. Look at your circle of friends and family. Are they helpers or hinderers? You want to be surrounded by helpers. They are the winners in life. Avoid the hackers who bring you down with their negativity or lack of support. As written in the good book, "iron is sharpened by iron; one person sharpens another" (Proverbs 27:17). To be sharp, be around sharp people. It's that simple. Ever hear your parents say, "Birds of a feather flock together"? It's important to be with the good flock! Being around good people who inspire and encourage you help you rise above the tough times.

Sean Patrick Tario, CEO of Open Spectrum, told me, "Don't go at it alone. Have a wise council. Your own executive board of mentors who share truth and wisdom with you openly. Talk with them often and be open-minded to their feedback. Seek advice from these people who can give you honest transparent feedback." The key point here is don't be a lone wolf. Have your own personal board of advisors who can give you good advice and are willing to give you straight feedback. Then make sure you're open-minded and open-hearted to embrace what they say and do an honest assessment of yourself to determine what you may need to change to make progress. Then do the work to make the changes you find as needed.

There are three keys to surrounding yourself with good people and making good of it all.

1. Identify who the good people are that you like to form a relationship with and then make effort to build that friendship.

2. Be willing to share your challenges and ask for help if needed.

3. Be open-minded enough to really listen and act on the wisdom shared to help you move forward in a better way.

Are you open to getting help? Are you open to finding good people to be around? Are you open to change? Knock and it will be given to you. Seek advice with a thirst to gain a new perspective to move you forward and you will find wisdom.

Craig Stone, CEO of Hire Networks, advised that one should "Ask for help from many sources like friends, family, and mentors. The key is to always be building your relationships through good and bad times. Lay the groundwork ahead of time so you're not only going to people during down times." It's wise to secure a good variety of opinions and feedback so you can have ample points of view for consideration. Take time to build and foster relationships in good times and bad, so you're not just going to people when you need them. It's key to always be a giver first and plant seeds of genuine love and support for others so if you ever need council or help, you already have built a solid relationship on which you can pull from and lean. It's like making a deposit into an emotional bank account. The idea is that each one us carries an emotional bank account in which we store acts of positive or negative emotions. We want to always make sure we're depositing more good emotions with our relationships so we have a positive bank account with people from which we can draw from when needed. In tough times it's then ok to ask your good surrounding friends and family for help.

Andrew Schwab, President of First Flight Venture Center, shared this wisdom on the importance of surrounding yourself with good people and being ok with asking for help:

> Recognize it's okay to share with people you trust about your personal life, fears, worries, and doubts. It's good to get this off your chest, but also people can relate and then also be there to truly help you. Don't go it alone. You are not alone. Everyone has been through struggles. Others may be going through something similar.

We need to remind ourselves that it's good to be open and authentic with people and not be fearful of opening up. It's in our opening up with others that we're able to draw closer to friends and family. And in this closeness, we are able to share more, support more, learn more, and ultimately love more.

They say the first key to intimacy is openness. The willingness and ability to be vulnerable. Being open with others allows your soul to shine and opens up the heart of others who

with their own humanity and empathy can re-
late to you and shine back support, love, and
care. The root of all depth in relationships in
authenticity and openness. The more real we
are with people the deeper our relationship develops and the stronger the bond.

Bob Witter, CEO of Device Solutions, went
through hard times losing two brothers before
the age of fifty-two, parents, and divorce all
within a short time span. His advice: "Seek wise
counsel. There is much wisdom in counsel. Ask,
who can I talk to? Do not be afraid to ask for
help and seek professional help." This made
me think of the wise proverb that says "plans
fail when there is no counsel, but they succeed
when advisers are many. . . . For by strategy war
is waged, and victory depends on many counselors" (Proverbs 15:22, 24:6). The more counsel
we receive from different sources the more clarity we can obtain. Sometimes life can throw a lot
at us that can be confusing. As they say, When it
rains it pours, so it's okay in these harder times
to be humble and recognize we may need help

both personally and professionally. And it's okay to ask for help. In our weakness we are strong. It's takes strength to ask for a hand to get up; we're all in this life together. You may be picked up today by someone, but tomorrow will be your turn to help someone else. It's all part of the circle of life. Just remember it's okay to ask for help when you're down as it allows others to be there for you, which is a gift to both of you.

In talking with Will Barfield, CEO of Barfield Revenue Consulting, he made it very clear how important it is to have a good group of people to associate with when going through adversity. Will noted:

> Rely on friendships and your network. Have a close circle of mentors to bounce ideas off of. Have an idea of what you want to know and what you're aiming for and then seek council. Most importantly, listen and be open to changing your thinking and adjusting as needed based

on the wisdom gained. And trust your gut and intuition too!

This reminds me of another area of importance when it comes to reaching out. I talked with entrepreneurs who we're in the gray area before launching companies, trying to figure things out. It was very common for them to go on twenty to thirty coffee or lunch dates in a month to seek advice from others. This kind of intensive networking or "Rising and Grinding" as known in the startup community, can give you a fuller perspective on what you may need to do or new direction you may need to take to achieve better results and/or march forward on a new better path. Like in a lab with any experiment you want to gather as many data points as you can to see patterns in the data set that help you draw the most sound conclusions. So talking with fifteen people versus five about something on your mind needing advice is 3x better in gaining more wisdom points to draw wisdom from.

Sumit Vohra, CEO of Lonerider Brewery, echoed this sentiment by sharing, "It's good to have others around you to share ideas and bounce ideas off. This helps you gain additional dimension and perspective. So surround yourself with good people and give back too. Respect. Listen and then do your best to do right by others." This is good advice as life is all about give and take. Sharing and caring. Then at the end of the day we have to do our best and do good for others and by others. No man lives on an island and more heads are better than one when making decisions. Tap the brain trust!

One of the golden themes throughout this chapter is to have positive people around you and don't be too proud to ask for help. Humble yourself and know it's okay to ask for support if needed. Asking for help does not mean you are less of a person or weak. Motivational speaker Les Brown says, "Ask for help, not because you're weak, but because you want to remain strong."

Overall it's important to be mindful of who you surround yourself with as people rub off on you, and we become — in both outlook and actions — a little like the people we spend the most time with. Negative people will weigh you down with negativity and positive people will lift you up with positive vibes, so choose the good kind of people to be around to help you keep moving up and becoming better and wiser. In life it's great to be a positive person to help others going through hard times so you're being a positive loving force in life. In addition your positivity attracts the right type of people in your life too. The best way to help yourself is to help others too. Serve and give back!

Chapter 2 Reflection

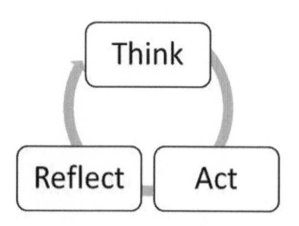

"Surround yourself with the dreamers, and the doers, the believers, and thinkers, but most of all, surround yourself with those who see the greatness within you, even when you don't see it yourself."
- *Edmund Lee*

What stands out fresh and distinctive to you from this chapter surrounding yourself with good people and asking for help?

How can you deal with adversity in a new way based on the teachings from this chapter?

45

CHAPTER 3

---❖---

KNOW WHAT YOU CAN AND CAN'T CONTROL

"*God, grant me serenity **to** accept the **things** I **cannot** change, courage **to** change the **things** I can, and wisdom **to know** the difference.*" —John Maxwell

It is important when going through hard times to understand what you can and can't control. Bottom line, don't sweat the small stuff. Do not worry about things you can't control. Worrying is like a rocking chair. It's give you something to do, but gets you nowhere. Why waste time thinking or fretting about something you have absolutely no ability to impact, like the weather? No matter what you do you can't make it rain or stop raining right? Just focus on things you can control like using an umbrella when outside in the rain or learning to dance in the storm. The key is to focus on the things you can control, like what you choose to do with the minutes of the day and what you spend your time focusing and working on.

In my research the biggest proponent for the importance of knowing what you can and cannot control was Dr. Steven LeBoeuf, President of Valencell. He suggested that you should "Focus on what you can control. Kind of like being a good student and getting good results in passing tests." I like this perspective because it reminds me of how you get good grades in school and the actions you can take to control the outcome of your class results. Simply focus on the things you can control, such as attending class, paying attention, asking questions, taking good notes, doing the homework, and then study, study, study many days in advance versus cramming the last minute. You can control these things, and thus control your class results: the kind of grades you get. Dr. LeBoeuf went on to further comment about this mind-set:

> Know the power you have to interpret and control your reaction to things. You can control how you view an issue. Be introspective and evaluate yourself. Then learn what needs to be changed, what you can change or not, and then be self-motivated to do it! In tough times realize how much ability you have to reframe your issue to solve the challenge. Know you have the power over yourself to make changes, see things more positively, and look for the good in all situations.

This is great advice in dealing with tough situations. I like how Dr. LeBoeuf summed up this point of view by sharing what his roommate told him in college, "Change the things I can and to hell with what I can't." This is straight to the point good advice. Don't sweat things you can't control. For the things out of our control, which is the majority of situations, the best advice is to let go, and let God. Just give it up to him because he's be up all night anyways. Pray and then work your prayers. Ask and seek wisdom, follow your heart, and put in the work you feel called to do that addresses your prayers. Then let go. Or as said in layman terms, do your best and then let the chips fall where they may. Trust the man upstairs.

Sean Patrick Tario, CEO of Open Spectrum, told me "The key is to recognize you have control and accountability for your actions and situation. The buck stops with you. When in hard times, take a moment to stop and ask the hard questions. Look in the mirror and use the challenge as opportunity to face yourself." This is a fresh way of suggesting the importance of doing a reality check and being honest with yourself about your situation to call a spade a spade so you can address the truth and heart of the matter. That is where real change occurs. When you recognize what need to be done, what you can do with your efforts, and the parts needing to be left to the powers that be

Sean Patrick Tarios' feedback is also good because it helps you realize the first step to overcoming and moving forward is recognizing your situation as a teachable moment and opportunity to learn. What can you gain from this situation? What is life trying to teach you? The one thing you have full control over is the way you view your situation and then the actions you take to address it. So be mindful and introspective of what lies within your hands and what is outside your sphere of influence. As "Everything matters," Dr. LeBoeuf said. And yet "everything doesn't'." In the grand scheme of things, it's important to keep the eye on the prize per what matters most in life and what you can effect. Don't dwell on the minutia. Be like a hawk and keep a birds-eye view on what matters in the world and keep a healthy perspective.

Chapter 3 Reflection

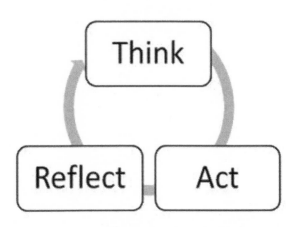

"You cannot control what happens to you, but you can control your attitude toward what happens to you, and in that, you will be mastering change rather than allowing it to master you."

- *Brian Tracy*

What stands out fresh and distinctive to you from this chapter about knowing what you can and can't control?

How can you deal with adversity in a new way based on the teachings from this chapter?

CHAPTER 4

HAVE PLAN, WRITE THINGS DOWN, AND TAKE YOUR FIRST STEP

If you don't know where you're going, then any path will take you there. You need to have a plan. A written strategy with clear goals you're aiming for and how to get there is a foundation for a great plan. The best way to plan and make your dreams come true is to write it down. There is something magical about writing down ideas that floats around in your head that makes them a reality. It's as if seeing your written plan documented moves the world to bring your idea to fruition. It's as if writing ideas down takes thoughts from your mind and crystallizes them into a gem you can hold. It's the spark that sets it all into motion.

Also, by writing down you plan, you can refine your thoughts to be more precise and on target with your goals. Your written plan becomes a living breathing document that grows and adapts with you. It can give you more clarity as you review it, and it can be updated as you gain more wisdom through many counselors. Leaders are readers and planers are writers. To make your dreams come true write down your aims.

In short, the first step to moving forward, upward, and onward especially in challenging times is to write down your plan: where you are, what your hope for, what do you want, what you would like to do, where you want to be, and how you see yourself emerging to new frontiers. Then write things you need to do to help set things in motion that move you toward your aim. This is the foundation of your plan.

A CEO who spoke highly about having a plan and writing things down was Mark Bavisotto, Founder of Successive Technologies and Startup Summit. Mark noted that "When facing issues, get everything down on paper. Look at it. Brainstorm ideas. Note things to overcome to obtain your aims and then start executing." One of the really good tactical items Mark recommended was journaling — a dedicated way to capture your writings. "It's great to have a journal," he advised. "One approach is to write down what you are grateful for, things you want to accomplish for the week ahead, and then note your bigger goals. It's great to journal your goals and personal accomplishments to help keep all moving forward and positive" This is great advice. Consider having a journal, so you keep all your thoughts in one spot. Having a guided outline for your writing like noting things you're thankful for and breaking up your goals into short and long term is worth a try, right?

Once you think of your plan and write it out, then take the first step. Do the thing you need to do to start moving toward your objective. Take the plunge! You have to move toward your goal to get your momentum going. Just do one of the things on your list that helps you get one step closer to your aim. Just do something on your list that you know helps you progress toward achieving your ambition. The key is action. Action begets more action and momentum brings about more momentum.

Sumit Vohra, CEO of Lonerider Brewery, is a big proponent of the paradigm for having a plan, writing things down, and taking the first step. He advised that you should:

> Recognize it first starts with you. You need to break down your problem. What is the problem and what do you need to do? Make a list and then just start that very first thing. Take one thing at a time. Note one item on your list and then act on it! That is how you get out

of adversity by doing simple things one at a time.

This approach is helpful as it really simplifies life's aspirations into small steps. By writing down what is important and organizing it into steps, you just have to take baby steps to accomplish the next item. Just do one thing. Anyone can take action on one thing; it's so very easy to follow this prescription. The good news is just doing one thing at a time leads to two things in motion or three things moving and then one spark leads to a bigger spark that results in a strong fire. Big things really are just a bunch of little things. The key is to focus on that one little thing you can do, and the world opens up and then you get the wind at your back.

On this view of a problem Sumit shared a silly question: "Do you know how to eat an elephant? One bite at a time!" Eating an elephant is a monumental task, but one that can be accomplished by taking one bite at a time; hence, take the first bite. Take the first step! The great thing is each bite or step takes you closer to accomplishing your aim. And each step forward gives you more momentum like moving down a hill. Some people call it the snowball effect. When you roll a little snowball in fresh snow, with just a few simple rolls that little snowball turns into a giant ball perfect, big, and ready for making a great snowman.

One of my favorite analogies on importance of taking first step and how it leads to great momentum pushing you toward accomplishing your goal is the flywheel effect. I read about this in the book *Good to Great* by Jim Collins. Here is summary based on this book giving great wisdom:

> Picture a huge flywheel—a massive metal disk mounted horizontally on an axle . . . weighing about five thousand pounds. Now imagine that your task is to get the flywheel rotating on the axle as fast and long as you can. Pushing with

great effort, you get the flywheel to inch forward, moving almost imperceptibly at first. You keep  pushing and, after two or three hours of persistent effort, you get the flywheel to complete one entire turn.

You keep pushing, and the flywheel begins to move a bit faster, and with continued great effort, you move it around a second rotation. You keep pushing in a consistent direction. Three turns ... four ... five ... six ... the flywheel builds up speed ... seven ... eight ... you keep pushing ... nine ... ten ... it builds momentum ... eleven ... twelve ... moving faster with each turn ... Then, at some point—breakthrough! The momentum of the wheel kicks in your favor, hurling the flywheel forward, turn after turn ... whoosh! ... its own heavy weight working for you. You're pushing no harder than during the first rotation, but the flywheel goes faster and faster. Each turn of the flywheel builds upon work done earlier, compounding your investment of effort. A thousand times faster, then ten thousand, then a hundred thousand. The huge heavy disk flies forward, with almost unstoppable momentum. Now suppose someone came along and asked, "What was the one big push that caused this thing to go so fast?" You wouldn't be able to answer; it's a nonsense question. Was it the first push? The second? The fifth? The hundredth? No! It was *all* of them added together in an overall accumulation of effort applied in a consistent direction. Some pushes may have been bigger than others, but any single heave—no matter how large— reflects a small fraction of the entire cumulative effect upon the flywheel.

The flywheel image captures the overall vibe of what it [takes for people overcoming adversity.] No matter how dramatic the ending action is, the great transformations never happened in one fell swoop. There was no single defining action, no grand program, no one killer innovation, no solitary lucky break, no wrenching revolution. Great change comes about by a cumulative process — step by step, action by action, decision by decision, turn by turn of the flywheel — that adds up to sustained and spectacular results. Bottom line, take that first step, and give that first push. Then push again. And again. It all starts there. Right now! (To learn more about this check out Jim Collins articles about the Flywheel Effect.)

Overall these three little methodical steps can make a world of difference. Have a plan, write things down, and then take the first step.

This is a good recipe for overcoming any adversity and helping you accomplish any aim. A simple thing to follow. You can do it!

CHAPTER 4 REFLECTION

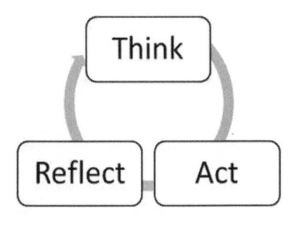

"By failing to prepare, you are preparing to fail."

— *Benjamin Franklin*

What stands out fresh and distinctive to you from this chapter about having a plan, writing things down, and taking your first step?

How can you deal with adversity in a new way based on the teachings from this chapter?

CHAPTER 5

DON'T GIVE UP

You never know how close you are to striking oil or finding gold. A good metaphor for life to encourage us to keep on keeping on. A mighty oak tree does not come down with one blow of an axe. It's the constant hits and continuous strikes, in which after persevering through many swings, that brings the big mighty oak tree down. Anything worth it in life is worth working toward and not giving up. First and foremost make sure whatever you're doing or aiming for is worthwhile and aligned with who you are and your unique gifts and talents. No use having a goal that is ultimately not good for you and then not quitting on something that is not going to ever produce good results. They say the definition of insanity is doing the same thing over and over again expecting different results. As important as it is to keep pushing on and not give up, it is just as important to know when to change course and pivot to better path.

One of the most stand-out perspectives on not giving up came from Andrew Schwab, President of First Flight Venture Center. He shared the wonderful concept of "Intersection of Opportunity." This is that special zone where hard work, luck, and opportunity all meet and the rewards come in. It's the right time, right place, and right moment when great opportunities come together. You want to make it to that intersection of opportunity! Andrew noted,

> You need to survive and advance. Keep at it long enough to reach that intersection of opportunity. It's hard to keep going, but you must persevere and keep trying. It's always easier to give up during a difficult moment, but pressing on often leads to that intersection of opportunity that was just around the corner. Remember, you don't know when the intersection of opportunity will arrive so must keep at it. . . . Never give up. Keep pushing yourself by getting in the mix and stay open to new opportunities. Get out of your comfort zone. Keep pushing toward your goals. If any obstacles get in your way, think up, around, over, or through to get passed it.

The intersection of opportunity is that special zone where hard work, luck, and opportunity all meet and the rewards come in. It's the right time, right place, and right moment when blessings come together. You want to make it to that intersection of opportunity! It's is perfect for the image presented at the start of this chapter. You never know if you're just inches away from hitting the jackpot. Perhaps it's that last ditch effort that is needed to hit gold. That's why everyone advises in the sports world to always dig deep. As Richard Nixon said, "A man is not finished when he's defeated. He's finished when he quits." So don't quit. One of my favorite quotes relating to this comes from a fortune cookie, "Fall seven times get up eight."

At the end of the day not giving up is really about tenacity and persistence. Be strong like bull! David Gardner, CEO of Cofounders Capital, talked to me about charging through, not giving up, and being a rhino: "Be like a Rhino: two-inch-thick skin, big horn, start running, and then knock things down in your path. As someone facing adversity, be a rhino who charges forward big bold and strong. This is what rhinos do, and this is how you succeed." I think it's powerful to remember the rhino analogy because in life we will all face tough weather and obstacles so have thick skin, a big horn, and run full steam ahead! As David continued, "Remember the rhino as inspiration. If you were a gazelle you would get knocked over, but as a rhino you stay the course and hard times are par for the course. If making it through to big accomplishments were easy, everyone would do it. Take the hits and keep going." This reminds me of that old Timex watch slogan, "It takes a lick and keeps on ticking." One of the best presidential quotes on the importance of persistence came from president Calvin Coolidge: "Nothing in this world can take the place of persistence. Talent will not: nothing is more common than unsuccessful men with talent. Genius will not: unrewarded genius is almost a proverb. Education will not: the world is full of educated derelicts. Persistence and determination alone are omnipotent."

Bob Witter, CEO of Device Solutions, captured the essence of not giving up simply by stating, "Don't give up. Know and see there is a light at the end of the tunnel. Go find it! Move toward something and keep moving. Instead of giving up, get up and ask, What do I need to work on? What can I do better? Then get up every day and move the ball forward. Nothing is insurmountable. Just take one step at a time".

When I joined Bigfoot Networks to head up retail sales for the gaming networking products I was living in San Jose, California. The company was based out of Austin, Texas, so I had to travel to their offices often. In the first weeks there I had to overcome a steep learning curve while also struggled with in my personal life. The travel back and forth made it harder on my wife. I was offered to move to Austin and my wife at the time did not want to move. I felt stuck between a rock and a hard place. Sitting in the parking lot in Austin office one early morning, I told myself I was going to just quit. Somehow from that moment to walking in and getting through the day I was able to move past that and hung in there. Thank God I did as a few weeks later the company announced they were opening an office near me in San Jose. I did not need to relocate. Then the best thing happened two years later. The company was acquired by Qualcomm, one of the best companies in the world. It was fruitful both financially and personally as I received an offer to work for Qualcomm. The point is if I would have quit I would have missed that great ride. Hang in there!

Bjorn Borg, a famous tennis player who was super tough on the court and known for grueling matches, said, "My greatest point is my persistence. I never give up in a match. However down I am, I fight until the last ball. My list of matches shows that I have turned a great many so-called irretrievable defeats into victories." I recommend you look up some highlight videos on Bjorn and Jimmy Connors, another tennis legend who never gave up.

If you want a simple mantra to live by, remember what famous NFL football coaching legend Vince Lombardi said: "Winners never quit and quitters never win." Hang in there! When the going gets tough, the tough get going! The key is to find balance, knowing when not to quit and when to move on. Ask for wisdom on this from your close trusted friends, mentors, and family — and pray. Then do what you're called to do!

CHAPTER 5 REFLECTION

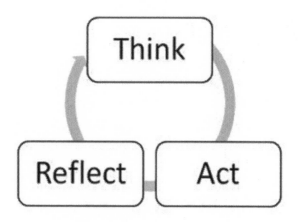

"Never give up, for that is just the place and time that the tide will turn."

—*Harriet Beecher Stowe*

What stands out fresh and distinctive to you from this chapter about not giving up?

How can you deal with adversity in a new way based on the teachings from this chapter?

CHAPTER 6

TAKE CARE OF YOU

YOU CAN'T POUR FROM AN *Empty* *Cup.* TAKE CARE OF YOURSELF FIRST

Copyright 2018 By Washo

E ver been on an airplane and heard the instructions of the crew talk about how to be safe during any emergency landing? They explain how the oxygen masks will drop down and how you need to put your mask on first before trying to take care of any children. The main point, and it's critical, is to get yourself safe first so you can then be able to help others. Well, so it goes in life. You can't be of any help to yourself or others if you're running on an empty tank. If you are not healthy you can't be healthy for others. You must be well nourished, rested, strong, and well to be any of those traits for others. Look in the mirror? Do you like what you see? Are you proud of you? If yes then others see you similarly. If you don't like what you see in the mirror then the reflection to others will be the same. Take care of you to be healthy and positive so you can then be strong and a light to others.

Chris Heivly, Managing Partner of The Startup Factory, told me how important it is to take care of yourself. He made it very clear that sometimes in life you need to take time to get away, refresh, and let go of things to recharge and come back with a fresh new perspective:

One of the things I learned going through hard times is how you need to take time to get away. Take a vacation. Step back and come back with a fresh clean slate. Wash and reboot. Come back anew so you can approach things with newness. Then enjoy new conversations with an open mind, open heart, and with no specific intentions. This allows the world to open up and for serendipity to emerge.

This refresh approach is about stopping the routine business of life to do something unique and different that focuses on newness and betterment of yourself. Take a vacation or get away specifically for special care of your health, physical body, mental fortitude, and spiritually, so you gain an extra boost in strength to get through hard times and face the real-world with a stronger spirit and renewed vigor. When interviewing Mark Steele, CEO of the SPMC Group, he made a big deal about putting your health first. He opened up about a new health benefit gained from overcoming some his hardest times at IBM, managing lay-offs and at startups raising capital and oversee-ing payroll for employees when cash was tight. He had to overcome vast amounts of stress and pressure that took him to the point of a serious health scare resulting in what seemed like a heart attack, but was actually just stress!

> The challenging IBM layoff experience taught me the importance of needing to step back and not be part of the process but to think differently and find new solutions. Be a problem solver and address issues in unique ways. Work backwards from the solution you hope to achieve and be rational. Most importantly, I learned that you need to take care of your own wellness first. Your health has to come first.

> You need to really take care of yourself. If you don't fill your well before your well runs out of water, it will dry up

at the worst time. Always fill your well (health, spiritual, love, wellness) to ensure you're full of goodness and energy to have fuel to get you through any challenging times.

This is great wisdom, specifically about ensuring your health tank is full before challenging times hit. Just like you need to fill your gas tank before that big car trip over the mountains. It's good to keep your health and wellness at the forefront of your daily routine so being healthy is more of a lifestyle versus a series of crash diets or short-lived health kicks. The old mantra "slow and steady wins the race" is great when it comes to maintaining everyday wellness. Take care of you daily and be mindful of your health meter like you are checking your gas tank every time you drive.

John Rosar, CEO of RevGen, recommended that

You must stop and smell the roses. Work hard and focus on your goals, but as important know your time slot and boundaries on when to focus on your personal life and health. Life is too short to stare at a computer screen. Make sure you're living a life of joy where you enjoy what you do at work, but also enjoy what you do outside of work. Ensure you give yourself the time and space needed to regroup and recharge.

This is wonderful wisdom around being mindful of your health and wellness by making yourself a priority. Schedule time for you and your personal joys outside of work. This is also good advice for living a well-balanced life and having a good work-life balance. Give time to your passions and joys. This will make you happier and healthier hence more joyful to face anything thrown your way with a more positive spirit.

CHAPTER 6 REFLECTION

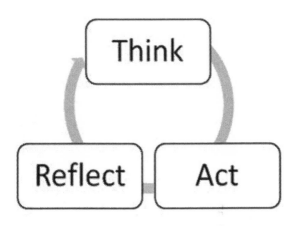

"You are a VIP, a very important person so take care with self care. If not you, who? If not now, when?"
– *Toni Hawkins*

What stands out fresh and distinctive to you from this chapter about taking time for you?

How can you deal with adversity in a new way based on the teachings from this chapter?

Part Two:

Fruits and Blessings

In this section you will learn how good things come from hard times. Blessings come from overcoming the trials of life, and they make us stronger and wiser. The song "Blessings" by Laura Story is about blessings that come through raindrops and healing that comes through tears. Sometimes it's the hard rains that bring forth the best soil and most fruitful new life.

You will learn about some examples of blessings these executives gained going through challenges, and how the hard times really did lead to great gifts later on that improved their personal life and professional career.

CHAPTER 7

WONDERFUL GIFTS AND NEW UNDERSTANDING

Sometimes some of the greatest gifts we get in life are those we cannot hold. Gifts of the heart and spirit lead us to being better people, smarter, wiser, and kinder. Many of the gifts the CEOs noted as the best blessing that came from overcoming hard times were character related. The most common character trait gained was empathy—the ability to be more empathetic, patient, and understanding of others.

As Andrew Schwab, President of First Flight Venture Center shared:

> Part of experience you gain from going through hard times is new perspectives. These challenging times can make you more humble and sympathetic to others. It can also make you a better person overall per being able to relate and have more of a "soft spot" for others going through hard times.

This is a good point. Once you walk a mile barefoot yourself, you can better understand someone else who is walking barefoot. By experiencing the feeling of going through a hard time you can have better understanding for what someone else is experiencing. That is the basis and foundation of empathy. Being able to feel and be there for another. Empathy is one of the best assets for getting along with others and being a good friend, servant, and leader.

In addition, getting through hard times gives us the blessing of just feeling better about ourselves. Overcoming an obstacle is a self-esteem builder. You feel great getting through a hard time. Kind of like running a marathon. It's a bit of a pain running it, but when you cross the finish line, elation sets in. Hallelujah! What a great feeling of accomplishment. That gift of joy comes in. Nothing worth having comes without a price, and some of our greatest blessings in life come through the hard times. As Dr. LeBoeuf, President of Valencell noted,

> Getting through hard times makes you much wiser. You feel better getting through it. . . . You become a better person. You are better able to put yourself in someone else shoes and have empathy. The earliest traces of this enlightening proverb dates back to the Cherokees who advised, "Don't judge a man until you have walked a mile in his shoes." You never really know a person until you understand things from his or her point of view. Until you climb into his or her skin and live in it.

The point is going through hard times, like a loss of someone you love, gives you that gift of heightened sensitivity to be there for others who experience a similar loss. Your ability to have greater empathy and sympathy makes you a better person, and in the end, you can feel better about yourself for that extra awareness in your character too.

Sometimes the gifts gained from hard times come in extra special and unexpected places. This was the case for Will Barfield, CEO of Barfield Revenue Consulting. He went through some hard times in personal relationships and lost his father too. However, through the challenges he had his three beautiful daughters and wife to rely on, and after losing his father Will gained a special perspective and added courage. "Among some of the blessings I gained," Will shared, "were even closer relationships with my daughters. I also have an incredible loving supportive wife who has helped me grow, reflect, and be a better person. Losing my father gave me a new perspective on what's important in life. It sped up my professional transition timeline and forced hard conversations at home and at work. Ultimately it helped me go for it when it came to launch my own company. I had a quiet talk alone with Dad, and I felt him. He and I both knew I was ready.

Life is full of twists and turns and it's wonderful to see beautiful things come out of ashes. Like in nature. For example, as we watch the hot lava reclaim wide swaths of the island of Hawaii, as tragic as it is, it will eventually lead to conditions ripe for a new forest bursting with new flowers. As Kerri Hall, CEO of MicMag by Me, noted, "God writes straight through crooked lines. Understand hills and valleys are a part of life. What comes through hard times are new paths and new gifts and talents. Hard times have led to a new better version of myself. During your dark times it can be your greatest opportunity to discover your purpose and true self. Use down times as blessings in disguise." This feedback really summarizes the essence of this book in how good things come from hard times. You just have to be conscious of the opportunities amidst the hard times

Mark Bavisotto, Founder of Successive Technologies and Startup Summit, shared some blessings he gained from getting through hard times: "One of the blessings to be gained in hard times is becoming a new person. A new creation. Learn to be less hard on yourself. A new form of gratitude emerges. You can become healthier and more confident having made it past obstacles. Getting through down times helps you gain a better growth mind-set too." Clearly, there are many examples of how hard times can be life's greatest teacher, showing us wisdom that results in good, how overcoming adversity provides a newfound sense of gratitude.

In my research on gratitude during hard times I found this poem by Troy Amdahl which captures the essence of what the CEOs shared:

Be thankful for the difficult times. During those times, you grow. Be thankful for your limitations, because they give you opportunities for improvement. Be thankful for each new challenge, because it will build your strength and character. Be thankful for your mistakes. They will teach you valuable lessons.

Another example of gifts gained from challenging times is how it makes you a deeper person. David Gardner, CEO of Cofounders Capital noted that:

> Hard times make you more soulful. They make you more empathetic and have more sympathy. They help you get closer to family. They make you reach out to people more and provides opportunity to slow down and become more humble. As they say, never waste a good depression. Use it to become more reflective and self-aware. You

really learn more about the importance
of patience. Learn and practice patience.

I liked what Arnold H. Glasow said about
patience: "They key to everything is patience.
You get the chicken by hatching the egg, not by
smashing it." It seems that we build our best
selves in terms of virtues and good character
when we pass through storms in our life. Craig
Stone, CEO of Stone Recruiting, shared how
hard times professionally led to a bigger stronger more diversified company that emerged
to better serve more markets, functions, and
verticals. With Craig having to go through cut
backs during the recession and losing good
people from his team to keep the company in
business he was awakened to the need to not
rely heavily on any one sector or service offer-
ing. Personally through the trial, Craig gained
a stronger faith in God and a better faith practice. "I became a more grateful person and
better father and husband," Craig told me. "A
more caring person overall. Going through
hard times gave me thicker skin. Seeing my

father go through health issues resulted in an awakening. Potentially losing him gave me a newfound energy and focus on being the best person you can be. Being a good light and rock to others like my Father was to me. I've learned to be humble and grateful. And be a lifelong learner." He is another good example of how you can learn and grow when going through the valleys in life. You just have to keep your eyes and ears open to the learning and be ready to make adjustments in your life that cooperate with this new understanding gained to deliver on a new you.

Remember the good fruit and blessing gained from going through hard times is new perspective on being a healthier you. As Chris Heivly, Managing Partner of The Startup Factory, shared, "One thing I learned through hard times is how important it is to take time and get away. The new appreciation for the importance of taking a vacation. This allows you to really step back and come back with a fresh clean slate. It's like a good wash or reboot that allows you to come back anew. This enables you to come back and approach all with newness and have new conversations with open mind and heart. Also, the importance of coming into new conversations with no specific intention to allow the world to open up and fate alongside serendipity to emerge." Taking time to get away is great advice as it's often in getting out of your existing environment to let yourself debrief on a vacation that enables you to come back with fresh eyes to see the world in a new light and have more patience with all as you let off some steam and decompress on retreat.

Mark Steele, CEO of SPMC Group, communicated a new health benefit gained from overcoming hard times at IBM managing layoffs and overseeing payroll for employees when cash was tight hence working to overcome vast amounts of stress. What emerged as a blessing for Mark having gone through this hard time was a new appreciation for better health, fitness, and ability to take care of his wellness.

Mark shared this insight, "Going through this hard time led to a better marriage and relationship by putting my family and my wife first. I also became a better leader by recognizing the tendency to be a workaholic not only in myself, but in my employees. This helped me better help others by modelling and allowing improved work-life balance."

Chris Heivly, Managing Partner of The Startup Factory shared some fruits and blessings gained from his more challenging times as gaining a healthier perspective on life noting, "I learned to not overreact. Not everything is a big deal. Don't sweat the small stuff. Also, be more curious and have wonderment for life. Life is a cumulative set of experiences so the more experiences the more colorful life."

The unique perspective on life's experiences — to recognize that this means both good and hard experiences — is enriching. Both good times and challenging times. This collection of experiences covers the full spectrum of emotions that leads to the most colorful rich life that enables you to be more fully alive, wise, and grateful for all.

Chapter 7 Reflection

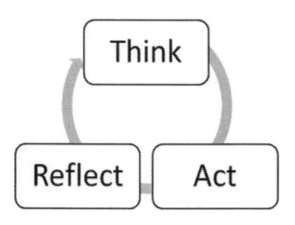

"Hard times are like a washing machine, they twist, turn and knock us around, but in the end we come out cleaner, brighter and better than before"

- Anonymous

What stands out fresh and distinctive to you from this chapter about the wonderful gifts and blessings gained from hard times?

How can you deal with adversity in a new way based on the teachings from this chapter?

FINAL CHAPTER: GOOD THINGS COME FROM HARD TIMES SUMMARY

The aim of this book is to pass on wisdom to help you get through hard times so you can move forward with a positive spirit to do more, be more, achieve more, and become a better person in the process. Hopefully by reading this book you have stronger faith and become stronger and wiser for getting through the valleys. Goodness awaits at the end of the tunnel. In addition, it is my hope that insights I've shared provide you a more lifted spirit and more opportunistic outlook for anything challenging you. Lastly, may the advice give you the tools needed to progress upward and onward toward greater success and new opportunities. This final chapter is a summary, the overall essence of the book. May these insights help you in your journey.

CHAPTER 8

❦

FOREVER CHANGED: BIGGER, BETTER, AND STRONGER

Hopefully by now you have embraced the overall message that good things come from hard times. That all challenges can be used for good and make us bigger, better, and stronger. Enjoy the keys summarized below to unlock your potential during any storms and implement the advice to push open new doors for you to achievement, joy, personal growth, and blessings.

- **Have a Good Perspective and Right Mind-set:** It all starts with a realistic perspective and healthy expectation that our life's journey truly is about ups and downs. We will have hard times and that is normal. Expect some valleys and when they come have the right mind-set to see them as par for course, and as some of your biggest opportunities for growth. Remember to "mine the valleys" to become wiser, stronger, and have new awesome doors opened up for you. Remember Rocky Balboa, "no pain, no gain." You got this!

- **Surround Yourself with Good People and Ask for Help:** You're the average of the five people you spend the most time with, so surround yourself with great positive good fun-loving people and you will become that too. Be in good company to be your best you. Having good wise people around you provides wise counsel you can count on for good guidance to get through any hard times. Lastly, remember it's okay to ask for help. When you are vulnerable with others, it gives them a chance to serve you, so you both benefit and the relationship deepens. By asking for help you will be blessed but then be prepared to help others in return when opportunity presents itself. Remember iron sharpens iron, so others are strong for you so you can be strong for others.

- **Know What You Can and Can't Control:** There is no better means for handling reality positively and no better mechanism for dealing with any situation in life more productively than knowing what you can and can't control and then to focus on things you *can* affect. The serenity prayer summarizes this best for us: "God grant me the serenity to accept the things I cannot change; courage to change the things I can; and wisdom to know the difference." To get through any hard time identify the things that need to change, the things you can control and impact, and then focus your time and efforts on taking actions take make a difference in your life. Everything else you can't control. Let go and let God.

- **Write Things Down, Have Plan, and Take the First Step:** What gets measured gets done. And writing things down helps you address the things on your mind, making your thoughts more real and actionable. Writing things down is therapeutic. It clears your mind, putting it at ease, knowing you took action to write down and examine your thoughts. The next step is to communicate your plan to a trusted "board of advisors," or friends. Remember the wise saying if you don't know where you're going, then any path will take you there. Have a plan and shoot for the moon because even if you miss you'll land among the stars. Lastly, once all is written down and consulted your board, take that first action to get something done. Just do something, anything on that list and plan. The action will beget more action and the movement will open up opportunities that bring about the results you're after. Like the flywheel effect the wheels in your life will get turning quicker and easier with the wonderful momentum that comes from every action you take. So just take the first step and eat that elephant one bite at a time!

- **Don't Give Up**: The problem with giving up too early or for wrong reasons is that oftentimes the moment you're about to quit is the moment right before the miracle happens. As Ross Perot said, "Most people give up just when they're about to achieve success. They quit on the one-yard line. They give up at the last minute of the game, one foot from a winning touchdown." The adage *fall seven times; stand up eight* is one of my favorite quotes for persevering. Stand tall another day. Give it another try. If at first you don't succeed try again. There will be times to give up or more productively put, to **pivot,** to something new. If you really did all you could and things are not working out and if after prayer you know in your heart it's time to move on to something new, then take action. The point is make sure you tried everything you could before you refocus. Go over, under, around, and through any obstacles first to ensure you gave your best to achieve what may be right on the other side of the door. Explore all options. Then if you do move on to pivot, you'll know you did everything you could, and it was time for change. You did not quit; you pivoted and did the right thing.

- **Take Care of You:** You only have one life to live, and you have a few brief years to shine and make a difference. Your greatest asset in life is you, your health, your spirituality, and your personal development in being the best version of yourself. To get through life in the best way possible, you have to make your health and wellness your number one priority. This is why having a good work life balance and taking time to keep yourself fresh and refreshed is super important. Taking time for your wellness will give you the energy and vitality needed to get through each day in positive spirits. Prioritizing your health will lead to success and joy for yourself and others around you. To be your best for others be the best for yourself. Take care of your mind, body, and spirit!

- **Have Faith that Fruits and Blessings Await You:** One of the best mind-sets to get through any challenges in life is to know that good things await on the other side of hardships. Hard times lead to great gifts whether here now, in the future, or heavenly gifts beyond our time here shall you believe in the other side. Just like storms and rains result in fresh earth, new life, and rainbows, the dark clouds we sometimes encounter in our journey result in new blessings. Remember when given lemons, make lemonade. Life isn't about waiting for the storm to pass, it's about learning to dance in the rain. So have faith and believe that good things are coming your way. There really is a light at the end of the tunnel so push through. As nothing great comes without some hardship. A beautiful brilliant diamond is just a piece of coal that stuck to its job! Shine on and know there is an amazing diamond in you being formed through the fire!

In conclusion, it's time for you to go forth! I'm confident with the implementation of the insights, wisdom, and advice shared you're going rise above anything in your way and shine your brightest light. I look forward to hearing about your success and new blessings showing that good things really do come from hard times. I'm here cheering you on and happy to support any questions or more information needed. Please contact me and share how you're doing at KeithWasho.com

About the Contributors

"No one who achieves success does so without the help of others. The wise and confident acknowledge this help with gratitude."

- Alfred North Whitehead

Here is a list of common traits these executives embody:

Hardworking, honest, straightforward, humble, confident, smart, fun, nice, strong, quick-witted, experienced, creative, good with people, strong listeners, funny, intelligent, proactive, get-it-done attitude, excellent communicators, effective, cool, calm, collected, wise, educated, responsible, respectful, generous, team players, disciplined, faithful, passionate, driven, adaptive, visionary, good listeners

Eric Wagner
Ceo Of Bruprint Brewing

Eric Wagner creates amazing craft brews from Bruprint Brewing such as Red White and Blue, which combines strawberry, blueberry and whit beer. Epic. Eric also serves the community in various capacities with his children and is an active member of his local church, Saint Andrews.

I have been fortunate to cross paths with Eric while visiting his beautiful craft brewery near downtown Apex, North Carolina. Eric is a wonderful host and greets you with a smile and treats you like family. Additionally, we crossed paths at church and quickly became friends.

Eric is one of those really nice down-to-earth guys in which what you see is what you get. He is humble and sincere and yet super smart and a thinker. What is amazing about Eric and his journey is how he left a good steady corporate job as an engineer to follow his dream to open up his own brewery and serve the community. He took a bold leap of faith and made his dream come true. Now Bruprint is one of the best and unique breweries in North Carolina. It provides a wonderful experience to people who visit his tasting room. Eric gave great advice about doing things for the right reason. Keep the big picture in mind. Do something you love and make a significant difference. If you ever want real-world wisdom on life, starting a business to follow your dream, and a deep dive on brewing, Eric Wagner is your guy!

Bob Witter

CEO of Device Solutions

B ob leads the highly respected engineering firm, Device Solutions, that offers feasibility studies, embedded hardware and software design and development, industry and carrier certifications and approvals, deployment services, and manufacturing support.

It was a blessing meeting Bob who was kind enough to welcome me to his Device Solutions offices in Morrisville, North Carolina, when I first moved to Raleigh. He gave an excellent view on the tech space in RTP. Bob also was one of the most candid, open, and kind interviewees. He was transparent, sharing some of his own personal struggles both in his business and personal life. What struck me most was his humble, kind nature in sharing advice and specifically how important it is to talk to friends, family, and trained professionals for anything challenging your dealing with. He made it clear, it's okay to ask for help.

Bob is a smart one and knows engineering, both hardware and software designs, and how to run a tech company like a pro. If you ever want straight-shooting good advice, both professionally in managing a company and personally in coping with challenges, Bob Witter is wonderful.

John Rosar
CEO of RevGen

John Rosar runs RevGen, an innovative outbound sales and staffing firm that develops sales individuals who represent the clients' customers through all interactions.

It was exciting to meet John, who is full of positive energy and a great giving spirit. He took time to meet downtown for lunch and provided a colorful recap on various tech companies and changes in the RTP region. John was also very open about some personal struggles both in business and personal life and had very vivid examples of what he learned and how has become stronger having gone through the adversity. What was great about John was how despite being super busy leading a fast-growing start-up he is very mindful of taking time for his health, personal life, and relationships. A wonderful example of someone who seeks a good work-life balance and keeps the activities of life in a healthy perspective.

Some of his favorite quotes are, "People need to be reminded far more than instructed." It's okay as a good leader to remind and reinforce key messages and aims to keep everyone on track. Also, "I never did a day's work in my life. It was all fun." Thomas Edison said this, referencing the importance of doing what you love and have passion for.

John is quick witted and clear thinking. If you ever want helpful wisdom points and guidance based on real-world experience all shared in a fun, friendly way like you're talking to a family member. John is fantastic.

Dr. Steven LeBoeuf

President of Valencell

Dr. Steven LeBoeuf is leading Valencell which is an exciting innovator in high-performance biometric sensor technology for wearables and hearables. LeBoeuf is one of those super charismatic guys that lights up the room with his fun, and witty personality. Being from a swamp about 50 miles southwest of New Orleans, I think he has one of the coolest accents in the world, and he tells colorful stories. LeBoeuf shared some of his challenges getting through all the universities, studies, and hurdles starting a new tech company. What was clear was his creative, can-do spirit when it comes to overcoming obstacles and being innovative in how he got through challenges. Some of the greatest things LeBouf shared was, "Leave no stone unturned. Always look for unique solutions to get things accomplished." And as important he said, "Believe you're here to make big things happen. Get outside your comfort zone. Good things come from stretching yourself and trying."

LeBoeuf is funny and a great guy that gives you that makes you feel like family. He is an amazing expert in all things wearable and hearable and knows biometric sensing inside and out with his work generating more than fifty patents in the field of accurate wearable sensors. He offers fantastic wisdom about launching a tech company and competing in the wearable tech space.

Mark Steele
President of SPMC Group

Mark Steele is at the helm of an international strategy and partnership consulting practice. Mark is a well-seasoned, smart, and kind guy with an amazing executive track record. He brings a wealth of life experiences having worked for various brands and tech companies both on the West and East coasts. We had some similar roots, having both worked for Qualcomm in California, and our paths crossed at CED (Council for Entrepreneurial Development).

What is great about Mark is his charismatic style and sincere interest in serving others. He is also super healthy, biking many miles weekly and staying active. Mark's good advice about succeeding in life, both personally and professionally, by ensuring your health is taken care of and that you think creatively around challenges was very clear. Remember as Mark said, "If you don't fill your well before your well runs out of water, it will dry up at the worst time. Always fill your well." Also, on being creative Mark noted, "Work backwards from the solution you hope to achieve." Be rational. It's important to step back and not just be part of the process. Think differently and find new solutions. Be a problem solver.

Mark is a great board member for Hunter Industries and avid volunteer. If you ever want to hear great stories about working for leading tech companies and lessons learned, Mark is super!

Mark Bavisotto

Founder of Successive Technologies and Startup Summit

Mark is a super entrepreneur with many activities in various companies, organizations, and conferences. He founded Successive Technologies US, Startup Summit in Raleigh, and is the director of Startup Grind Triangle. In addition, Mark is a great family guy with a wonderful wife and kids.

What is great about Mark is his down-to-earth, straight-shooting style. He is transparent and honest in everything he does. He is a strong proponent of journaling, writing down what you're grateful for each day. Capture what you want to accomplish for the day and week. Then list your bigger goals. And most importantly, think positively and celebrate your wins.

If you want to learn about how to wear many hats, start a company, and then give it your all to succeed both professionally and personally. Mark is a great guy to talk with who is packed full of experiences.

Andrew Schwab

President of First Flight Venture Center

Andrew Schwab is the top man at First Flight Venture Center (FFVC) in Durham. FFVC is one of the nation's largest and most stable incubators, hosting more than thirty-five high-science, high-impact companies annually. In total, FFVC company startups number more than 285 and growing.

Andrew is very articulate and a strong leader who is very well respected in the tech community. He is also very personable. Having experienced ups and downs in his career makes him humble and kind. One of his wonderful points of wisdom was the concept of persevering long enough to reach the interaction of opportunity in which the fruits of your efforts finally blossom. As Andrew noted, "Survive and advance. Live long enough to reach the intersection of opportunity. Sometimes it's hard to keep going, but you must persevere and keep trying. By not giving up you can reach that intersection of opportunity that may be just around the corner."

Andrew was generous with his time, meeting me to offer advice about moving to Raleigh-Durham and supporting me in writing this book by sharing advice on getting through hard times. His empathy on relating to others is fantastic and with his involvement in so many startups, he is pro on what to do and what to avoid.

Craig Stone

CEO of Hire Networks

Craig Stone provides strategic recruiting, staffing, and executive search services to blue chip, international, and emerging-growth companies.

Craig is one of those super polished well-rounded professionals who holds himself in high regard. He is very active in the community, both attending company events, local organizations, conferences, and serving the church. He is also a great tennis player and family guy who makes time to keep a good work-life balance.

What is nice about Craig is how well connected and kind he is. Craig is always so open to sharing introductions and generous with his time. He is also a seasoned pro in career development and the intricacies of hiring. When it comes to personal development in your career and doing good things in your personal life, Craig is an all-star!

Kerri Hall

CEO of MicMag by Me

Kerri Hall is an innovator in the furniture industry at the intersection of technology, buying trends, and furniture.

I met Kerri at NC Idea during her work in launching the new company and working on sales and marketing angles. Kerri is a very creative, smart, and passionate person with a big heart for all she does both professionally and personally. What stood out to me was her love for her kids and family. It was clear she was working with purpose to help others, serve, and be a good role model and contributor for her family.

It was great hearing about Kerri's strong faith and her openness to share it while helping other get through challenges. Kerri always sees the silver lining. Kerri is an all-star in the furniture industry and a strong woman with a great entrepreneurship spirit. She is full of great wisdom and a proud mother and great family member that puts' life into perspective wonderfully. If you're ever seeking information about furniture, business, and life, Kerri is a shining star.

Will Barfield

CEO of Barfield Revenue Consulting

Will Barfield owns a firm providing talent acquisition and placement, training, and consulting services in the areas of sales and recruiting.

Will is a wonderful person who looks like he played professional sports. He holds himself like an athlete: well spoken, disciplined, straight shooter, and hard-working.

What is special about Will is his story about taking the leap of faith to start his own company. He talks about how life is full of wonderful second chances and new opportunities to do great things. He is a great guy who loves his family and takes pride in his solid relationships with people. If you ever like to have a personable chat about life, baseball, staffing, and working full-time while starting a company. If you need hiring and career support, he is also one of the most well-connected people in the Raleigh-Durham area.

Sumit Vohra

CEO of Lonerider Brewery

Sumit Vohra makes some awesome craft brews distributed in nine states. Lonerider is counted among the top 150 breweries in USA, an Inc. 5000, and CED Top 25 winner.

Sumit is the kind of person who speaks softly but carries a big stick. He is super talented, coming from humble beginnings to excelling in school and then achieving in a great tech career. And then remarkably he pulled a big pivot to launch his own company and growing it to one of the most respected breweries in America.

What is great about Sumit is despite all his success and wonderful accomplishments, he is super kind and down to earth and always open to meet or talk. He truly believes in giving back and helping others. Some of his strongest advice was to be kind to all and follow your own path and to be the best version of yourself. If you want to learn about starting a company, the intricacies of brewing, and most importantly, how to do all in good spirit, lookup Sumit and Lonerider Brewing.

David Gardner

CEO of Cofounders Capital

David Gardner leads the most innovative startup accelerator focused on B2B software ventures in the Triangle. David hosts a lab space for entrepreneurs who receive expert help modeling and vetting their startup ideas, prototyping, and garnering beta customers.

David has an amazing track record of successes and a colorful life journey. He has a master of divinity, and was once a pastor, but also has a master of information science. He has held multiple leadership roles at various tech companies. In addition, he serves on many boards and advises numerous start-ups. He is also a great writer and provides awesome quotes and stories that illuminate his advice. You can read some of his work on Tech Wire from WRAL.

David was kind to host me at his offices in Cary and provided excellent feedback on getting through challenges and having the right mind-set for rising above down times. One of his most vivid examples he shared was the "be a rhino" analogy per the importance of taking some hits in life and keep moving forward with no fear and with strength like a rhino. David also explained that life is full bumps in the road so if you encounter some rocky points that means you're on the right path. David is a great guy both professionally and personally. He is also a very compelling speaker. David is a great person to meet who will be the highlight of your day.

119

Chris Heivly

Managing Partner of The Startup Factory

Chris Heivly manages the most highly capitalized technology accelerator in the southeast that runs a three-month program customized for early stage startup companies. He was also the founder of one of my favorite companies, MapQuest.

Chris is a highly versatile and creative person and is open to new opportunities and mixing it up. He wrote an awesome book that is fun and super informative: *"Build the Fort: Why 5 Simple Lessons You Learned as a 10 year-old Can Set You Up for Startup Success"*

What is super about Chris is his giving spirit. He is open to sharing his wisdom from founding MapQuest to leading numerous companies. You can actually book time on his calendar by going to his website heivly.com for his monthly calls that are open to anyone. Awesome! Chris is super fun to talk to and he shares great wisdom with a smile and wide-eyed enthusiasm. Some of his greatest advice was the key to stepping back and taking a break in any struggle, so you can come back with new outlook and refueled enthusiasm to take on life with a more open-minded and positive spirit. Chris is kind and like family to converse with. I recommend Chris for any great chat about life, business, relationships, and most importantly fort building!

Sean Patrick Tario
CEO of Open Spectrum

Sean Patrick Tario owns and operates a consulting firm that sits at the core and heart of the data center industry. They also work as outsourced CTOs and CIOs when it comes to assessing how to architect and implement the infrastructure needed to support a company's business. Sean also leads a great podcast, "*I Love Data Centers.*"

Sean is a wonderful interviewee because he is such a deep thinker, good soul searcher, and speaks very kindly and directly from the heart with a well-formed conscious. His advice around being real with yourself and doing an honest assessment is very helpful for overcoming adversity and providing a reality check on your situation. Sean also was keen to share about how important it is for your family and partner to be in your decisions because teamwork and spouse cooperation is key to your success.

One of his great quotes shared was "to be, rather than to seem." He communicated well the key in aligning what you believe yourself to be, how others view you, and your ideal version of yourself. Sean is a super accomplished executive; I admire his risk taking in starting companies. What also makes him extra special is his wonderful focus on faith and family too. He is fun loving great father and husband. A one-of-a-kind great guy. Lastly, he is one of the most knowledgeable people in the world when it comes to the data center industry. If you ever need wisdom on that space and juggling all professionally and personally, he is your man!

IMAGE CREDITS

All Images & Illustrations© 2018 by Keith Washo.

About the Author

Keith Washo resides in Research Triangle Park, North Carolina, after nearly two decades of working in Silicon Valley for leading technology companies and startups. He is the published author of the *Heart of Success, Growing Your Professional and Personal Life in the Right Way* and has been honored by Toastmasters International as an award-winning contest speaker. He shares in a U.S. patent for digital audio players and is the founder of a consumer electronics business. In addition, Washo is a keyboardist, composer, and publisher of music. He holds an executive MBA from Saint Mary's College of California, a master's in music business and entertainment industries from the University of Miami and a BA in broadcasting and music from the State University of New York at Oswego. You can learn more at KeithWasho.com.

88330488R00087

Made in the USA
Middletown, DE
08 September 2018